OLD NORTH COUNTRY BRIDGES
UPSTATE NEW YORK

An Album of Historic Spans of Wood, Iron and Wire in Northern New York State

Compiled by
RICHARD SANDERS ALLEN

1983
North Country Books
18 Irving Place
Utica, New York 13501

Copyright 1983
by Richard Sanders Allen

ISBN 0-932052-28-2

All rights reserved
No part of this book may be
reprinted without written permission
of the copyright owner
First Edition

Manufactured in the United States of America
by Canterbury Press, Rome, New York

North Country Books
18 Irving Place
Utica, New York 13501

Old North Country Bridges

For 175 years the covered bridge has been an American landmark. Today it has become increasingly difficult to find even one, but less than 50 years ago the traveler was apt to encounter dozens of them in small towns and at country crossings from Maine to Mississippi; and as far west as Oregon, California and even Alaska.

But covered bridges in upstate New York? One salesman who drives thirty thousand miles a year in the north country has never seen one, and another can vaguely recall coming upon, —well, maybe two.

In the region roughly defined as "The Adirondacks," or "The North Country," comprising a seventeen-county area north and northwest of Albany and the Mohawk River there are still a handful of covered bridges. All their locations can be readily spotted; seven of them still standing in northern New York State, and all well over a century in age.

Five of these upstate covered bridges continue to serve on public highways, one is by-passed and preserved and one has always been private property. New York's quota of roofed spans is not and was never as large as that of bridge-rich Pennsylvania and Ohio, nor did the area ever approach the concentration of covered crossings to be found in sections of neighboring Vermont. Still, in the North Country region were and are structures from every period of the history of covered bridge engineering, and examples of most of the major patented designs.

First off, the inevitable question comes up.

"Why on earth were these bridges *covered*?"

Covered bridges didn't get built because they afforded a convenient refuge for horse-and-buggy travelers caught in a sudden summer shower. These sheltering portals were not to neatly shape a load of hay, or to prevent horses from shying at the sight of a wind-rippled sheet of water. And though their shadowy confines made an excellent place for sedate Victorian hugs and kisses, they were certainly not created for that express purpose.

The simple reason for covering wooden bridges was to protect their interior supporting timbers or "trusses" from moisture. Seasoned wood beams that result from years of exposure to air, but not damp, actually gain in strength. The roof, the side-boarding, even the floors were replaceable, but it was vital to protect the trusses, or "bones" of the bridge from wet and eventual certain rot.

The village bridge as it existed in nineteenth century upstate New York was the meeting place of town and country. In its dim interior men argued crops and politics while their womenfolk exchanged gossip and recipes and their children ogled the gaudy circus posters that still hung in the bridge long after the show had left town.

Out in the country a covered bridge was a good place to save a load of hay during a thunderstorm. Farm boys climbed in its rafters and found favorite fishing spots in its welcome shade. It sometimes seemed as though a high-spirited mare could actually *read* the signs that were prominently posted over the bridge portals: "Five Dollars Fine for Riding or Driving Faster than a Walk on this Bridge."—for often as not she would automatically slow to a sedate pace on coming in sight of the cool, dim timbered passageway. For years the covered bridge was country cousin to the big city amusement park's "Tunnel of Love." Just ask grandpa why they called them "kissin' bridges!" The longer the spans, the better.

In the early days of civil engineering, upstate New York was once a proving ground of bridge-building. Big and little spans were thrown across streams from Rouses Point to Remsen and from Albany to Alexandria Bay. There are records of nearly 300 covered bridges in the state, with well over a third of them in the North Country. The biggest and most important crossings were those of the Hudson and Mohawk Rivers and their tributaries.

Dominant in early New York State bridge building was Theodore Burr of Oxford in Chenango County, where he had come as a pioneer from Connecticut. Burr's spans were the first to be erected at such places as Utica, Little Falls, Canajoharie, Schenectady and Waterford. Built in 1804, this last was the prototype for hundreds of other "Burr Arch" bridges from Maine to the mid-West. They were a favorite of the early turnpike companies. Double-tunnel, Burr-type covered bridges were a common sight at major river crossings.

The first settlers of the Adirondack/North Country brought their bridge designs with them. The lattice-type bridge, invented by Ithiel Town of New Haven, Connecticut in 1820 was by far the favorite. Duplicating bridges with which the builders were familiar in their native New England, the Town lattice appeared across streams in the northern tier of New York State counties and in the Saint Lawrence Valley.

With the coming of railroads, turnpikes fell into disuse. But the weight of the iron horse occasioned a whole new generation of bridges and bridge-building. Though it is difficult to conceive today, the expanding network of steel rails made use of hundreds of wooden bridges, many of them roofed and weather-boarded even though this made them more vulnerable to locomotive sparks and loose ashpan spillage. It was because of railroads that the transition was made from wooden to iron bridges.

Pre-eminent as a bridge for railroads was the Howe Truss, invented by William Howe (uncle of the sewing-maching inventor) in 1840. Though for the most part wood, it had iron rods which could be adjusted and tightened at will as the wood shrunk, or when it shook loose under the vibration of passing trains. Howe bridges were built on the New York Central, the Delaware & Hudson and the Rome, Watertown & Ogdensburgh, to name only a few of the roads. Bridge components could be loaded on a couple of flat cars and readily transported to the erecting site; it was the first "pre-fabricated" bridge, in days before the term was used.

Of related interest, much of the history of iron bridges has to do with developments in the North Country. Squire Whipple of Utica devised both an iron bridge for railroads and a popular bowstring iron arch for use on the Erie Canal. Whipple's 1847 book was the world's first scientific approach to bridge-building ever published, and its influence made bridge-building a real profession. Other builders turned to the spanning of rivers by means of wire cables. Though never numerous, some early North Country suspension bridges were structures of long life and landmark status.

With the passing of the years and with floods, fires and highway improvement projects, the old bridges have disappeared, one by one.

Prior to World War II there were over fifty covered bridges in New York State, plus a number of old iron spans of importance to engineering history. A few still stand, their existence precarious at best.

But for the rest, only old prints and photographs remain to put in the mind's eye a picture of the days when wood, iron and wire put North Country travelers from one bank of a stream to the other.

NOTE:

The following assemblage of old pictures were extracted from the author/compiler's collection of some 35,000 items relating to the history of bridges and bridge-building.

For ready reference and usage the illustrations are organized alphabetically by county.

Where known, picture sources are acknowledged, and thanks are extended to all those who in any way have aided in the research. Without the help and generosity of literally hundreds of contributors to a lifetime's store of information, the compilation of this book would have been impossible.

—R.S.A.

On what is now U.S. Rt. 20, west of Sharp's Corners in the Town of Guilderland was this "double-barrel" Town Lattice bridge on the Western Turnpike. It was built c. 1840 with the guidance of Guilderland Town Road Commissioner J. P. S. Van Auken.
ALBANY COUNTY   Cr. Town of Guilderland Photo Bank

The Western Turnpike Bridge over the Normanskill served travelers and farmers bound for Albany markets for four decades. With the decline of turnpike travel, the narrower passageway was sometimes fenced off and used as a pig sty. Bridge was replaced in 1919–20.
ALBANY COUNTY
Cr. Wilson Collection

Northeast of Guilderland Center, spanning the Norman's Kill, was the French's Mills or "French's Hollow" Bridge. Built by Henry Witherwax in 1869, it replaced a previous open wooden bridge destroyed in a freshet. Bridge truss was 162'8" long by 14' wide.
ALBANY COUNTY   Cr. Basil Kievit Coll.

French's Hollow Bridge was a rare example of the Haupt Lattice Truss, devised and patented by Herman Haupt of Gettysburg, Pa. in 1839-40. As shown in this photo taken during demolition in 1933, the Haupt lattice timbers all slanted to a center post, and in this bridge were assisted by laminated arches.
ALBANY COUNTY   Cr. Basil Kievit Coll.

Southwest of Albany, the New Scotland Road was carried across the Norman's Kill on a neatly-kept, white-painted covered bridge with open wooden approach spans at either end. Instead of the usual stone abutments, the bridge stood on heavy timber supports. It was replaced c. 1910–11.
ALBANY COUNTY Cr. John V. B. Gerling

There were very few covered bridges over the Erie Canal. Just north of Watervliet this structure spanned the famous waterway between Locks #4 and #5, on a road leading to the John L. Thompson Chemical Works, (today's Elm Street). The Town lattice styling and details such as the end buttressing are similar to bridges erected by Joseph Hayward of West Troy (Watervliet) in the 1840's, and this one may well have been his work.
ALBANY COUNTY   Cr. Richard McBain, via Colonie Town Historian

Built as the entrance to a private home, the small Waldbillig Bridge adheres to the principles of structural engineering used by 19th Century builders. Erected in 1953 by Albany contractor Gerald Waldbillig and his son Michael, it spans Vly Creek off Johnson Road in the Town of New Scotland.
ALBANY COUNTY   Cr. Howard C. Bogue

The Normanskill Farm Bridge at the southwest edge of the City of Albany is another fine example of the rare Whipple "iron arch." This one was built at an unknown location in 1867 by Simon De Graff, a Syracuse contractor who probably built the type under an agreement with inventor Squire Whipple. Moved to this site c. 1900, the bridge is now privately-owned.
ALBANY COUNTY   Cr. R. S. Allen

Spanning Fox Creek at the hamlet of Waldenville, this lattice structure was reportedly build under the direction of General Hiram Walden, Road Commissioner c. 1830.
ALBANY COUNTY　　　　　　　　　　　　　　　　　　　　　Cr. Allen Coll.

Usually called "The Green Island Bridge," a long continuous covered structure stretched across the Hudson River, connecting the City of Troy with Green Island. It was originally built for the Rensselaer & Saratoga Rail Road (D&H) in 1835, as the first railroad bridge across the Hudson. It consisted of ten spans on eight piers, 1,616 feet of bridge. 1,700,000 feet of lumber went into it. Of patented Town lattice construction, the bridge was built by Isaac Damon of Northampton, Mass., and Joseph Hayward of West Troy (Watervliet). One lane served railroad trains and the other

vehicular traffic. The continuous structure was later divided at Starbuck's Island in midstream in order to provide access to an iron foundry.

Sparks from a locomotive ignited the eastern section of the bridge at noon of a Saturday in May, 1862. The resulting conflagration destroyed 507 buildings in downtown Troy. Replaced in kind, the two sections of the Green Island Bridge continued to serve both trains and wagons until rebuilt with iron in 1879 and 1884.

ALBANY-RENSSELAER COUNTIES   Cr. Allen Collection

Described as "a startling accident," and with good reason, the Albany & Vermont locomotive "Jay Gould" backed out of the open draw of the Troy-Green Island Bridge and ended up in the Hudson River. The date was Saturday, September 23, 1865.
ALBANY-RENSSELAER COUNTIES   Cr. Allen Collection

An important crossing of the Mohawk River at Cohoes carried both a highway and the towpath of the new Champlain Canal. A five-span Town lattice structure, the first of its type in the area, it was built in 1825–26 by Isaac Damon of Northampton, Mass., and Joseph Hayward of West Troy (now Watervliet). Badly damaged by ice in 1832, it was destroyed by fire in March, 1853. Painting by William Guy Wall looks east.
ALBANY-SARATOGA COUNTIES   Cr. Harry Shaw Newman Gallery

Another view of the first Cohoes covered bridge across the Mohawk River shows the State Dam and the famous axe manufactory of Daniel Simmons. This 1820's sketch by G. Hayward looks west.
ALBANY-SARATOGA COUNTIES
Cr. New York State Museum

A later version of the Cohoes highway-towpath bridge across the Mohawk River was a rare wood-and-iron "combination bridge" on the plan of Simeon S. Post of Jersey City, N.J. 695 feet long, of five spans, it was built in 1872 by the firm of Belden & Gale of Syracuse.
ALBANY-SARATOGA COUNTIES
Cr. Allen Collection

Built for the Albany Northern Railroad (D&H), this bridge was their crossing of the Mohawk River at Cohoes. 938 feet long, its six spans of wooden arch trusses were completely built of white pine and white oak. The bridge top was decked and trains trundled across the roof from 1857 to 1878.
ALBANY-SARATOGA COUNTIES
Cr. Allen Collection

A well-constructed Howe Truss covered bridge was built over the Ausable River at Keeseville about 1856. It was unusually long for the type; two hundred and fourteen feet in a single span. After two decades, under the weight of a three-foot snowfall and the onslaught of high winds, it collapsed during the winter of 1875.
CLINTON-ESSEX COUNTIES   Cr. Maurice Turner Coll.

The ill-fated covered bridge at the upper crossing of the Ausable River in Keeseville was succeeded in 1878 by a handsome two-span iron structure. Skilled workers journeyed from Pennsylvania to erect it, and their cast shields are still in place over the embellished portals. They read: "Murray, Dougal & Co., Builders, Milton, Pa."
CLINTON-ESSEX COUNTIES   Cr. R. S. Allen

Workers, together with spectators on the upper bridge at Keeseville pause to have their handiwork recorded on a tintype. Today, the Ausable River at Keeseville is spanned by an old iron bridge, a suspension foot bridge, and a venerable stone arch, all over a hundred years old.
CLINTON-ESSEX COUNTIES   Cr. Maurice Turner Coll.

A century and a half ago, Keeseville, with its forges, grist, woolen and rolling mills, nail and tool manufactories, looked like it might become the "Pittsburgh of the North." Here it was decided to permanently bridge the Ausable River with an arch of sandstone. When nearing completion the bridge was undermined by the river, but builder Soloman Townsend persevered and the "keystone arch" that he and his workers finished in 1843 has weathered time and the Ausable ever since. The view was drawn in 1857.

Just visible above the dam beyond the stone arch is one of a succession of workers' foot bridges across the Ausable River, the earliest on the suspension principle and hung from huge forged chains. Precarious at best, it was locally called "the Swing bridge." During a period of high water, a muster of the New York State Militia was held in Keeseville on September 13, 1842. The militiamen, accompanied by admiring citizens and small boys attracted by the screeching of fifes and the roll of drums, started marching across the bridge. They were apparently ignorant of the fact that a measured cadence of troops in step can be disastrous to any bridge. And so it proved at Keeseville. There were forty people on the swing bridge when the upper chains gave way, and thirteen lost their lives in the swollen river.

CLINTON-ESSEX COUNTIES   Cr. Allen Collection

1843 Stone Arch, Ausable River, Keeseville, N.Y.

Photo 6/75: R. S. Allen

Despite the tragic accident of 1842, additional pedestrian bridges on the suspension plan continued to serve Keeseville. The most recent, with wire cables, built by the Berlin Bridge Company of East Berlin, Connecticut, has been in place over the Ausable River since 1888.
CLINTON-ESSEX COUNTIES   Cr. Allen Collection

1888 Suspension Foot Bridge at Keeseville, N.Y.
Photo 6/75: R. S. Allen

In 1856 the East Branch of the Ausable River went on a rampage, carrying out nearly all the bridges along its course. At the village of Jay a new structure was built in the following year, by George M. Burt, total cost was $1500.00, a substantial 150' Howe Truss single span. The photograph shows the west bank connected by a further covered approach span of 80'. This was eliminated in the 1950's, and the original long main span reinforced by three concrete piers. Jay Bridge is today the only covered bridge still standing in the Adirondack/Champlain region of New York State.

ESSEX COUNTY

Cr. John L. Warner

With three lattice spans over the St. Regis River, the covered bridge at Hogansburg was the northernmost of its type in New York State. It stood from 1862 to 1931.
FRANKLIN COUNTY   Cr. John L. Warner

West of Chateaugay was a high arched covered bridge over the Chateaugay River, south of today's U.S. Rt. 11 leading to Malone. This river, to the north just over the line into Canada, still flows under a covered bridge at Powerscourt, Quebec.
FRANKLIN COUNTY   Cr. H. I. Doud

Over the Little Salmon River at the village of South Bombay was a small lattice bridge with projecting portal overhangs. It was reportedly built in 1876 by Town Highway Superintendent John Congdon, and a Mr. Aiken. The bridge served the village for 72 years, being replaced in 1948.
FRANKLIN COUNTY
Cr. John L. Warner

A spectacular 150-foot housed wooden railroad bridge once carried the old Northern Railroad at Malone. On high masonry abutments, it perched 82 feet above the gorge of the Salmon River. The bridge was built by the Northern's superintendent, Col. Charles L. Schlatter, in 1850. Col. Schlatter used a modification of the old Burr Arch plan, devised by another well-known bridge and railroad engineer, Henry R. Campbell of Philadelphia, Pa. and Burlington, Vt.
FRANKLIN COUNTY   Cr. Allen Collection

Osborn's Bridge is now a watery ghost town deep beneath the waters of the Sacandaga Reservoir, or "Great Sacandaga Lake." Built by John Patterson, the long, two-span Town Lattice bridge that gave the village its name stretched its bulk across the river from 1840 to 1930; ninety years.
FULTON COUNTY   Cr. Allen Collection

At the site of Sir William Johnson's old "fish house" on the Sacandaga River was an early fording place. Here, in 1818, a sizable covered bridge was erected. It was on the Burr kingpost and arch plan, with three spans of 125' each. Contractor for the building of the bridge was young Daniel Stewart of Luzerne, who used an appropriation from New York State of $5000. Stewart's big bridge stood for 112 years. Then it, and the nearby village of Fish House (or Northampton) were "drowned out" by the filling of the Sacandaga Reservoir in 1930.
FULTON COUNTY
Cr. Howard L. Humes

Interior of the Fish House Bridge shows the massive construction involved in the Burr Arch plan, with traffic lanes separated by a set of center trusses. Advetisements plastered on the rafters were a common sight in almost every covered bridge. When this century-old veteran was floated off on the rising waters of the Sacandaga Reservoir the timbers were salvaged and put to good use in many neighborhood buildings.
FULTON COUNTY   Cr. Howard L. Humes

25

A little west of Fish House (Northampton) stood the Vlaie Creek Bridge, over the stream draining the great swamp called "the vlaie." The first bridge here, built in 1835, was burned in 1883. This long Town Lattice span replaced it, and like its downstream neighbors over the Sacandaga, was flooded out by reservoir waters in 1930.
FULTON COUNTY   Cr. Allen Collection

On Fulton County's western border is Emmonsburg. This was once a busy village devoted to the tanning industry, with its own covered bridge over East Canada Creek. Holcomb's tannery is long gone, and the bridge was replaced in the 1880's.
FULTON-HERKIMER COUNTIES   Cr. Anita Smith, Montgomery Co. Historian

Dolgeville was called "Brockett's Bridge" until the 1870's. It was a two-span king post/arch structure erected over East Canada Creek in 1829–30. After Daniel Dolge built felt mills here the crossing continued to serve the burgeoning industrial village until 1893.
FULTON-HERKIMER COUNTIES   Cr. Allen Collection

Hamilton County's only covered bridge spanned the Sacandaga River at the north end of the village of Wells. Originally high above the stream, it had two spans and was of Town Lattice construction. The building of a dam and the resulting Lake Algonquin put the water level perilously close to the lowers chords of the bridge, but it survived until replaced by a new state highway bridge in 1932.
HAMILTON COUNTY

—Eastern Illustrating Co.

North of Herkimer on the road to Middleville, the curving West Canada Creek passed under "Dempster's" or "Countryman's" Bridge, a three-span Burr arch structure. The bridge debouched directly on a railroad crossing and was the scene of several accidents. Replacement came in 1921, and relocation of today's Rt. 28 has eliminated this crossing of the creek.
HERKIMER COUNTY   Cr. Allen Collection

Northwest from Salisbury on the German Church Road, this 49-foot covered bridge spanned Spruce Creek. Alvah Hopson used a modified Burr Arch and kingpost plan in erecting it c. 1875. It succumbed to high water in the 1950's.
HERKIMER COUNTY   Cr. R. S. Allen

A mile east of Salisbury, on what is now State Rt. 29, Spruce Creek once tumbled over the rocks below this small single-span kingpost and arch bridge of the type built locally by Alvah Hopson. It was once known as "Moore's Mill Bridge."
HERKIMER COUNTY   Cr. Allen Collection

Still standing on Mechanic Street in Salisbury Center is the last of the town of Salisbury's six covered bridges. A 42-foot Burr arch truss span, it was erected c. 1870 by Alvah Hopson, the man who is credited with the design and building of most of the area's roofed crossings. Spruce Creek's waters formerly turned the wheels of numerous small mills and local industries. Once called "Elwell's Falls Bridge," the Salisbury Center structure is still passable, and is maintained as an historic landmark by the town.
HERKIMER COUNTY   Cr. Jack L. Mowers

Typical of the small Spruce Creek covered bridges of Salisbury, this one stood east of the Dolgeville Road about a mile and a half south of Salisbury Center. Since this is "Hopson Road," it is likely that Salisbury's covered bridge builder, Alvah Hopson, had a hand in its erection. Replacement came in 1926.
HERKIMER COUNTY   Cr. Allen Collection

A local landowner named Fink gave his name to the suspension bridge which once spanned the Mohawk River east of Little Falls. Two railroads and the Erie Canal converged on the constricted gorge of the Mohawk River here, where Fink's Bridge was a mid-nineteenth century link to connect all the East-West traffic.
HERKIMER COUNTY   Cr. Allen Collection

The Mohawk Turnpike, which connected Schenectady and Utica, ran along the north shore of the Mohawk River, and had many toll houses strategically located where traffic had to converge to cross tributary streams. This was the case west of St. Johnsville, where the 'pike bridged East Canada Creek. The three-span, double-barrel Burr arch covered bridge here was very old, purportedly dating from 1812, and may even have been designed by the inventor, Theodore Burr, himself. It was replaced in 1912 after a century of service, by an early concrete arch bridge, which today is by-passed and crumbling.
HERKIMER-MONTGOMERY COUNTIES
Cr. St. Johnsville Enterprise/News

A covered bridge in the service of the lumber companies once stood at Gang Mills (now Hinckley). Possibly of the rare unpatented Whipple wooden truss design, with arches, the bridge spanned West Canada Creek in the 1870's.
HERKIMER-ONEIDA COUNTIES   Cr. Howard Thomas Coll.

"Trenton Falls," a deep gorge through which West Canada Creek tumbled and twisted, was once a prime tourist attraction. The Falls were bridged east of Prospect by this high, single-span covered bridge with arched trusses.
HERKIMER-ONEIDA COUNTIES   Cr. Howard Thomas Coll.

Known as "Cameron" or "Cameron Hill" Bridge, this single span over West Canada Creek was built, along with the road leading to it, in 1849. The design was an unpatented creation of bridge inventor Squire Whipple of Albany, better known for his iron trusses. When the Cameron Hill Road to Gravesville was abandoned, this rare type of covered bridge was purposely burned in the spring of 1937.
HERKIMER-ONEIDA COUNTIES   Cr. Basil Kievit Coll.

Between Poland and Trenton State Route 28 crosses and re-crosses the wide West Canada Creek. At the junction of today's Rt. 8 was this covered bridge, apparently a Howe Truss structure of single span.
HERKIMER-ONEIDA COUNTIES
Cr. Henry M. Lanpher

An early crossing of the Black River in Watertown was the long Town Lattice covered bridge on Court Street. It was replaced by an iron bridge in 1883.
JEFFERSON COUNTY   Cr. John L. Warner Coll.

"Log London," facetiously named for an early wilderness settlement, was in the Town of Ellisburg. Today only ghosts of its cheese factory, shoe shop and scattered housing are to be found northwest of Pierrepont Manor. It stood on the banks of the South Branch of Sandy Creek, which was spanned by this covered bridge. In this sleepy backwater, when this photograph was taken in 1907, little attention was being paid to the stencilled admonition on the portal: "$15 Fine for Riding or Driving on this bridge faster than a Walk."
JEFFERSON COUNTY
Cr. Bert Steele

At Allendale, in the Town of Lorraine, this single-span Town Lattice bridge spanned the South Branch of Sandy Creek. It was condemned and replaced c. 1910.
JEFFERSON COUNTY
Cr. Allen Collection

Copy of an old stereo view shows the "Bradford Suspension Bridge" which spanned Black River on Mill Street in Watertown. This 175-foot bridge was devised and erected in 1857 by Gilbert Bradford, a Watertown machine tool and steam engine manufacturer. Being familiar with 5/8" thick boiler plate, Bradford utilized it for the 17½-foot iron towers. From these he hung ½" dia. wire cables, forty feet above the Black River's North Channel.

Bradford's Bridge was much admired by a writer of the day, who declared it to be: "a monument to (the builder's) energy and ambition." Another stated that: "it will endure till an earthquake . . . or the corroding tooth of time shall destroy it." It was indeed time's tooth which finally caused replacement of Gilbert Bradford's unique suspension bridge in the 1890's.

JEFFESON COUNTY   Cr. Smithsonian Institution

At the former lumbering village of Lyonsdale, the Moose River was diverted to saw mills. It passed under a wooden bridge, with one open span and one covered. Tumbled logs and sawdust piles dominated the scene at the turn of the century.

LEWIS COUNTY   Cr. Allen Collection

St. Johnsville had a covered bridge across the Mohawk River, connecting the village with the Erie Canal on the south shore. Apparently a two-lane, latticed, toll bridge of three spans, it stood from 1841 to 1897.
MONTGOMERY COUNTY Cr. St. Johnsville Enteprise/News

To cross the Mohawk River from Nelliston to Fort Plain, a big, two-lane Burr arch toll bridge was erected in 1828. Subsequent to 1857 a free bridge, built on the Whipple iron bow-string plan was built alongside it, which appears in this picture, taken in 1861. After the toll company gave up, the two bridges were used in conjunction. Surprisingly, the wooden bridge outlasted the iron one, which was gone by the 1880's. Barely visible in the picture are the short-lived iron trusses and, in the distance, another covered bridge over Otsquago Creek at the eastern edge of Fort Plain village.
MONTGOMERY COUNTY Cr. Allen Collection

An artist's drawing of 1857 shows Fort Plain Bridge across the Mohawk River, with a New York Central train passing the combined railroad station and hotel in the foreground.
MONTGOMERY COUNTY   Cr. Allen Collection

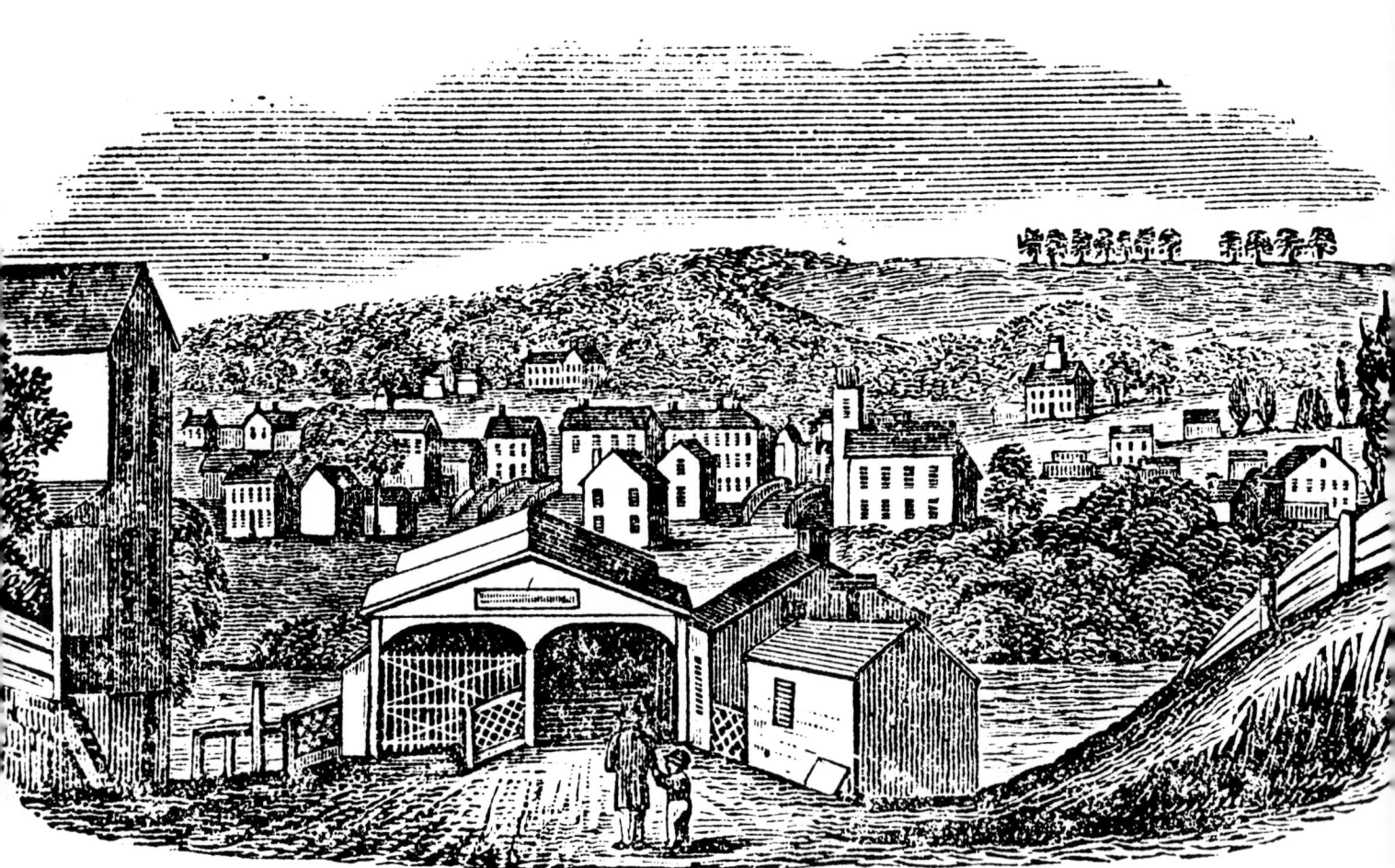

Eastern view of Canajoharie.

The original bridge at Canajoharie was a single-arch, built in 1803 by Theodore Burr, "the celebrated wooden bridge builder." This was not one of his better creations, for it collapsed in 1807. The site was also known as "Palatine Bronk's Bridge," and from this came the name for the north shore village. The third bridge here, a two-lane covered one, was erected by the Canajoharie & Palatine Bridge Company about 1826. When the Schenectady & Utica Railway was built, the bridge had the roof and floor of its north span raised to clear the tracks with an overpass. Later, because frequent high water covered the flats on the Canajoharie side, two iron Whipple truss spans were added. The old covered portion was destroyed by fire in 1901.
MONTGOMERY COUNTY   Cr. Allen Collection

An enlargement from an old print of 1845 shows the Caughnawaga covered bridge across the Mohawk River at Fultonville. Built in 1824, it had three spans and a double lane passage. A road across the flats connected the bridge with the "Caughnawaga House" and depot on the north or Fonda side. A new lattice bridge here was under construction in 1865. On St. Patrick's Day of that year two canal boats washed out of the basin at Canajoharie and came down the swollen Mohawk River. The first took out the center section of Caughnawaga Bridge and the second the south span.
MONTGOMERY COUNTY   Cr. Allen Collection.

A New York State Legislative Act to incorporate the "Fort Hunter Suspension Bridge Company" was passed on April 7, 1852. The bridge was designed by John W. Murphy, a twenty-four-year-old graduate of R.P.I. A crew from John A. Roebling's Wire Works reportedly came up from Trenton, N.J. to string the long cables across the Mohawk River in 1853. After four decades of service the bridge was dismantled in 1935.
MONTGOMERY COUNTY   Cr. John A. Bennis Coll.

Amsterdam and Port Jackson, its Erie Canal suburb on the south shore of the Mohawk, were connected by a three-span Town Lattice covered bridge, built in 1843. The north span was ripped out in 1865 by the floating center section from the Caughnawaga Bridge upstream, and replaced by iron.
MONTGOMERY COUNTY   Cr. Allen Collection

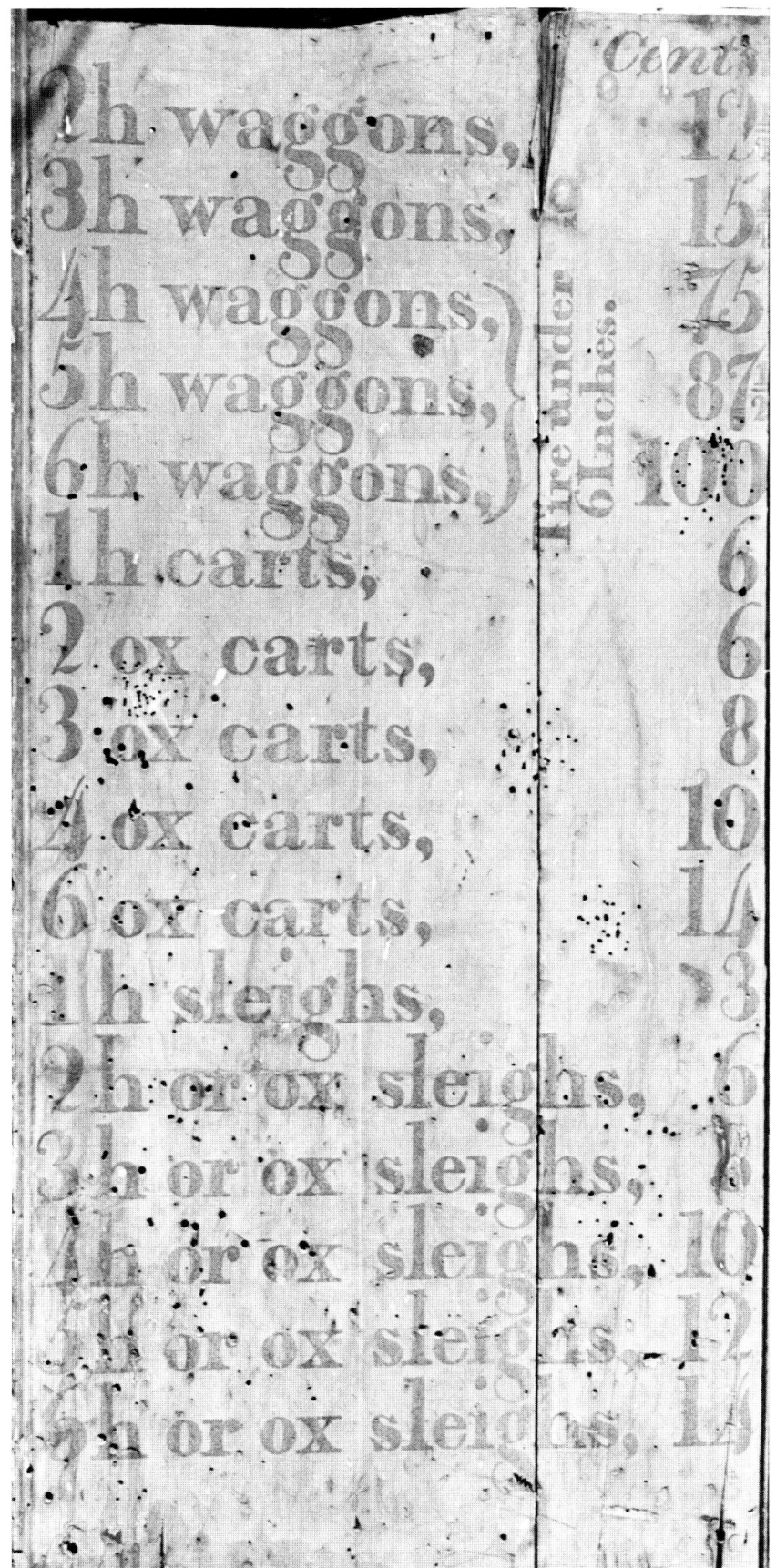

Toll Board of the old covered bridge which once crossed the Mohawk River at Amsterdam.
MONTGOMERY COUNTY   Cr. William D. Mohr

Most highway and private bridges over the Erie Canal were framed wooden or iron spans, the former not being roofed. An exception was a covered canal bridge which served the extensive farm property of Henry Silmser, in the Town of Glen, near Fultonville.
MONTGOMERY COUNTY　　　　　　　　　　Cr. Anita Smith, Montgomery Co. Historian

Until its destruction by an ice jam on March 22, 1948, this was Montgomery County's sole surviving covered bridge. Called the "Whitlock" or "Wagner's Hollow" bridge, it was 71 feet long. It spanned Caroga Creek to the west of Ephratah, and was situated in the Town of Palatine.
MONTGOMERY COUNTY   Cr. R. S. Allen

Even rarer than covered wooden bridges are some of the early iron truss spans still standing in isolated locations of Northern New York. Among these may be counted a small Whipple truss bridge over Cayadutta Creek just north of Fonda. This private bridge, well over a century old, is thought to have originally stood at the old Thompsons & Richards Paper Mill, a short distance upstream from its present location. The cast iron arches, splayed at their bases, serve to readily identify the "Whipple" type.
MONTGOMERY COUNTY   Cr. Robert M. Vogel

Inventor Whipple left no doubt as to the origin of his patent bridge truss, as evidenced by his name cast into the segmented arch of the Cayadutta Creek Bridge near Fonda. Squire Whipple (1804–1888), of Utica and later Albany, has rightly been called "the father of iron bridges," and was the writer and publisher (1847) of the first scientific work on bridge-building in America. Squire (his given name), patented his "Iron Arch Truss Bridge" in 1841, and these structures were built by the dozens for over thirty years.
MONTGOMERY COUNTY   Cr. Robert M. Vogel

Squire Whipple's iron bow-string truss bridges were an everyday scene as the standard road bridges erected to span the Erie Canal. The State of New York pre-empted the truss design "for the common good," and the inventor received little recompense for his efforts. In a rare instance of rightous indignation he declared: "These little bridges I invented; rats get the pay!" This view of 1866 of a Whipple truss over the Erie Canal at Canajoharie looks north toward Palatine Bridge over the Mohawk River.

MONTGOMERY COUNTY   Cr. John Bennis Collection

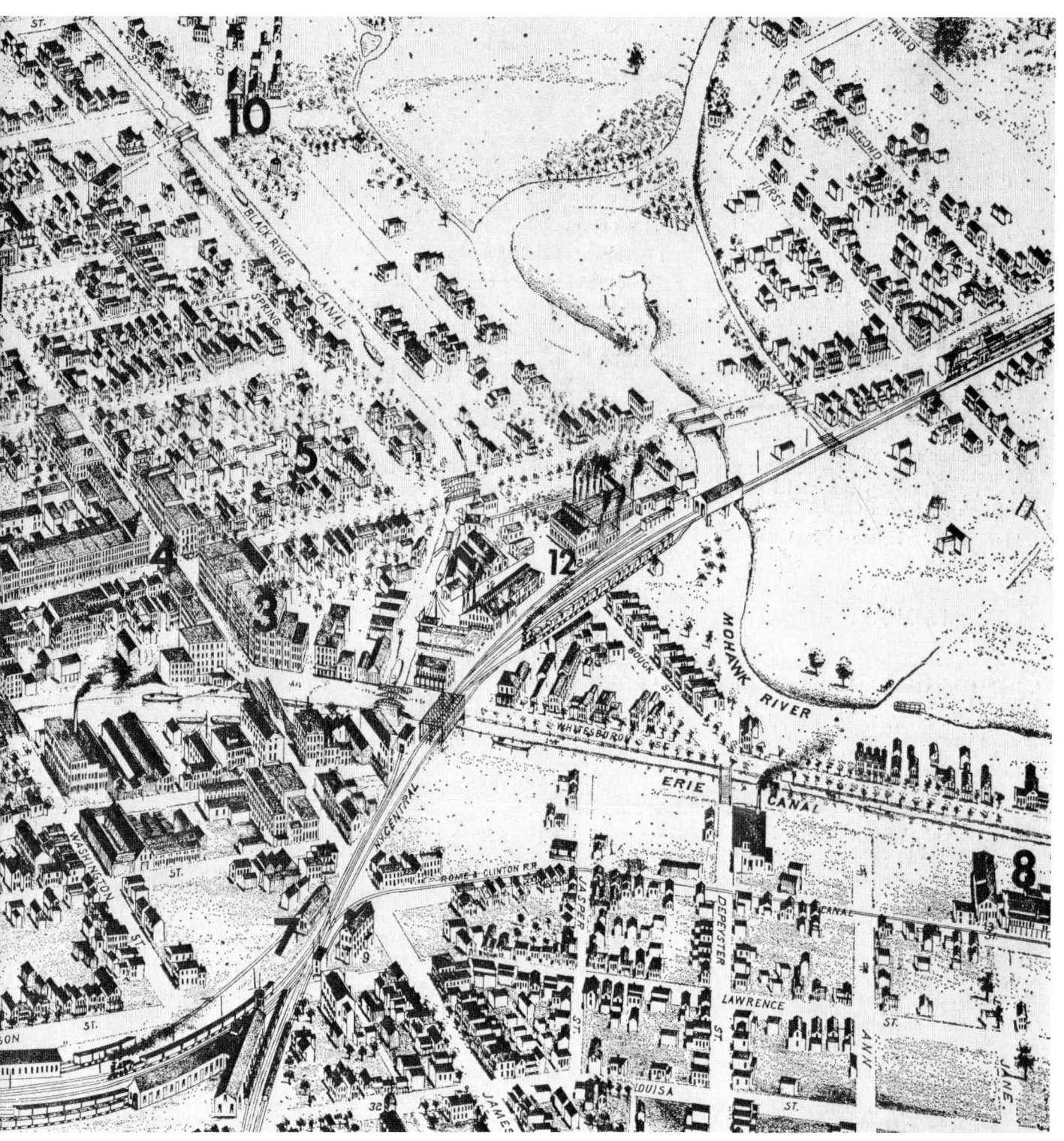

In an 1873 Bird's Eye View of Rome, a double barrell, two-span covered railroad bridge can be seen (lower right) serving the main line of the New York Central. It spanned the Mohawk River adjacent to the Rome Iron Mills (No. 12).
ONEIDA COUNTY   Cr. Rome Sentinel

This simple king-post covered bridge crossed Cinncinnatus Creek on what is now N.Y. Rt. 12 north of Remsen.
ONEIDA COUNTY   Cr. John L. Warner Coll.

Well known to travelers between Troy and Bennington was the "Big Hoosic" covered bridge on N.Y. Rt. 7. A solidly-built, double Town lattice truss, it had odd "flying buttress" type supports built over auxiliary abutments, making it a four-span structure. Built in 1840, it stood for 90 years. In 1930, a new, high-level Hoosic River crossing was built to the south, and only an overgrown causeway and a few stones in the river remain to mark the old bridge site.
RENSSELAER COUNTY   Cr. Warren Broderick Collection

Over a slough of the Hoosic River west of Hoosick Village was the "Little Hoosic" covered bridge on N.Y. Rt. 7. When its larger counterpart was demolished in 1930, this bridge was kept as part of an access road. Unhappily, the hurricane-flood of 1938 lifted "Little Hoosic" bodily from its abutments and smashed it into an adjacent field.
RENSSELAER COUNTY
Cr. Allen Collection

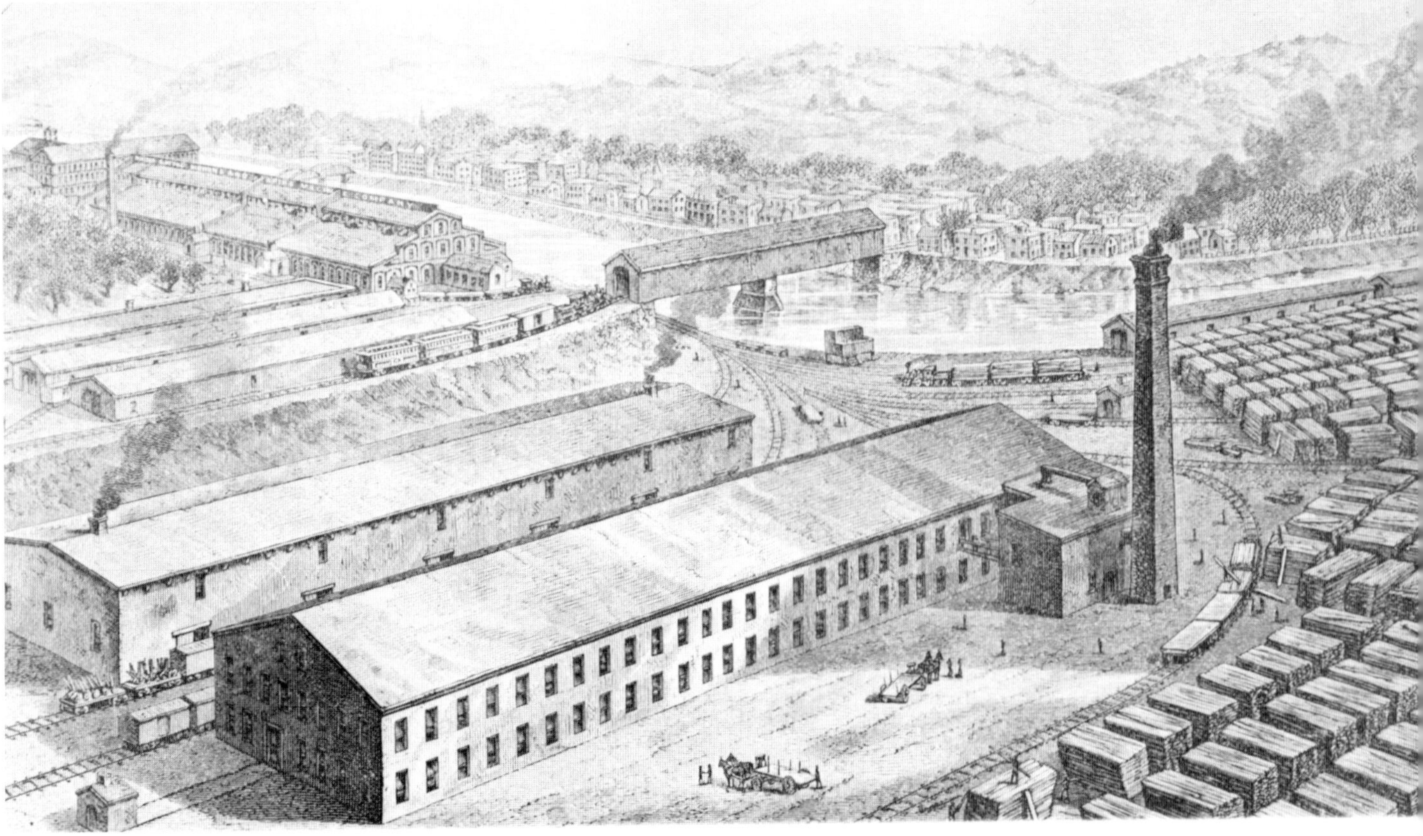

North of the two-level railroad depot at Hoosick Falls stood this two-span covered railroad bridge over the Hoosic River. Erected by the Troy & Boston (B&M) Railroad, it was replaced in the early 1880's. The bridge is here shown surrounded by the one-time giant industrial complex of the Walter A. Wood Mowing & Reaping Machine Company.
RENSSELAER COUNTY
Cr. H. F. Eastman Coll.

This covered bridge once spanned the rocky gorge of the Little Hoosic River, as well as a mill flume, at the village of Petersburg. It was a single-span Town lattice structure, on the route of today's N.Y. Rt. 2, the Taconic Trail. Replacement of the covered span came in 1911.
RENSSELAER COUNTY
Cr. Allen Collection

The lower crossing of the Little Hoosic River at Petersburg was a longer single-span Town lattice truss, known as "Well's Bridge." A concrete arch replaced it in 1911.
RENSSELAER COUNTY   Cr. Warren Broderick Collection

Just east of North Petersburg, the Little Hoosic River joins the main stream of the "big" Hoosic. Just south of its mouth was a single-span, horizontally-sided Town lattice bridge. A new state highway structure on what is now N.Y. Rt. 346 replaced it in 1922.
RENSSELAER COUNTY   Cr. Allen Collection

North of Schaghticoke Hill, on the main road (N.Y. Rt. 40) from Troy to Schaghticoke, the Tomhannock Creek was spanned by a Town lattice covered bridge with auxiliary external and internal arches. Replacement came in 1920.
RENSSELAER COUNTY   Cr. Warren Broderick Collection

"Primitive" American artist Thomas Wilson painted this landscape with the village of Eagle Mills, in the mid-nineteenth century. The short, double-barrel covered bridge in the center of the hamlet spanned the Posten Kill.
RENSSELAER COUNTY   Cr. Abby Aldrich Rockefeller Folk Art

Shedd's Bridge was located on the former main highway, east of the Bennington Battlefield in the Town of Hoosick. Built about 1850, it had every hope of completing a century of service. Unfortunately, during renovation in 1947, a jack used to prop it up was stolen. On retrieval from the Walloomsac River, the bridge's lower chords were found to be broken beyond salvage and repair.
RENSSELAER COUNTY   Cr. Broderick Collection

A flood-weakened abutment of the covered bridge at North Hoosick gave way c. 1910, sending one truss of the latticed span crashing into the Walloomsac River.
RENSSELAER COUNTY   Cr. H. Lee Hull Collection

This unique covered bridge once spanned—not a river, but the main line tracks of the Boston & Maine Railroad on 101st Street in Troy. It was a covered wooden overpass, built in 1885 as a new entrance to the Oakwood Cemetery. The bridge was ornamental as well as utilitarian, a 94-foot Howe Truss structure set on a noticeable skew. The portals had black decorative panel timbers and rounded shingles, painted a dark green. At one time the bridge sported two iron-railed outside sidewalks. Despite corrugated top and bottom sheathing, fire destroyed the "Cemetery Bridge" in 1963.
RENSSELAER COUNTY   Cr. John L. Warner

A scene never again to be duplicated. A Boston-bound Boston & Maine passenger train rumbles out of Troy under the Cemetery Bridge of 1885-1963. At the time that this unusual structure was destroyed by casual vandalism, it was the very last covered wooden overpass in the United States. Today at this entrance to the Oakwood Cemetery there are no trains, no tracks and no bridge.
RENSSELAER COUNTY Cr. Gene Baxter

Both Albany and Troy were in hot railroad competition for the commerce of Western New England. The capital city's contender was the Albany Northern Rail Road, built in 1853. The rails crossed the Hudson River north of Waterford by means of a long all-wood bridge; eight spans of arched trusses. The Albany Northern (later Albany Vermont & Canada RR) was too strapped for money to ever roof or weatherboard their bridges, and after only six years usage the line was abandoned from Waterford to Eagle Bridge. Historian-artist Benson J. Lossing made this, the only known pictorial representation of the short-lived bridge, about 1858.
RENSSELAER-SARATOGA COUNTIES   Cr. Allen Collection

The Derrick Swart House, depicted by Benson J. Lossing in the 1850's, still stands today. Little is known of the long covered bridge which crossed the Hudson River at Stillwater. A toll bridge, it was erected in 1832 and destroyed by an incendiary fire in 1875.
RENSSELAER-SARATOGA COUNTIES   Cr. Allen Collection

One of the earliest of covered bridges in the United States, this was a four-span, 797' structure over the Hudson River between Lansingburgh and Waterford. Here, in 1804, famed bridge builder Theodore Burr first put his patented "Burr Arch Truss" into use.
RENSSELAER-SARATOGA COUNTIES Cr. Allen Collection

After 105 years of existence, the "Union Bridge" between Waterford and Lansingburgh was destroyed by fire on July 10, 1909. Leaking gas from a main laid beneath the bridge was ignited from sparks made by a passing trolley car.
RENSSELAER-SARATOGA COUNTIES   Cr. Allen Collection

This big, two-lane Burr arch covered bridge over the Hoosic River was built in 1827 by the Hoosick and White Creek Bridge Company. Early on, a local hunter shot an eagle and to boast of his prowess, nailed it up on the portal face of the bridge. The name "Eagle Bridge" stuck, and the dead bird was eventually replaced by a painted eagle. An iron bridge (complete with iron eagles which still are attached to the present steel bridge) succeeded the covered bridge in 1898.
RENSSELAER-WASHINGTON COUNTIES
Cr. Allen Collection

An old, two-span covered bridge spanned the Hoosic River on the main road (now N.Y. Rt. 346) between North Petersburg, N.Y. and North Pownal, Vt. It was replaced by a steel structure in 1920. Though always called the "State Line Bridge," the vagaries of boundary surveying geographically put all but a corner of this bridge in Vermont.
RENSSELAER COUNTY, N.Y.-
BENNINGTON COUNTY, VT.
Cr. Allen Collection.

Connecting two counties, and the last of its kind remaining over the Hoosic River is Buskirk's Bridge to the north of N.Y. Rt. 67 in the scattered village of Buskirk. The original primitive wooden structure here was built in 1804 by Martin Van Bushkirk and successor spans have all borne his name. Today's covered bridge at Buskirk, a 136-foot Howe truss, is the fifth on the site. It is thought to have been erected c. 1880 using timbers from an earlier bridge of 1850. It is painted a barn red with white trim, and still bears the admonition neatly painted on its portals that there is a stiff fine "for driving faster than a walk."
RENSSELAER-WASHINGTON COUNTIES   Cr. Raymond Brainerd

The interior of Buskirk's Bridge demonstrates that all covered spans are not alike. This bridge uses the Howe Truss, a panel system of wooden cross-members and iron-rod verticals. It was devised by William Howe, a Massachusetts housewright, in 1840, and was the standard American railroad bridge for over three decades.
RENSSELAER-WASHINGTON COUNTIES   Cr. Henry A. Gibson

A substantial covered bridge to span a tiny rivulet. This Town lattice bridge stood at Massena Center, over Kinney's Creek. It was built c. 1868 by Harry F. Crooks of Massena Springs, and replaced in 1930.
ST. LAWRENCE COUNTY　　　　Cr. John L. Warner Collection

A sturdy Town lattice covered bridge spanned the West Channel of Grasse River at Canton. Neat extra boxing protected the all-important ends of the wooden chords where they rested on the laid stone abutments. The bridge was built in 1863 and replaced in 1904.
ST. LAWRENCE COUNTY   Cr. John L. Warner Collection

A single-span Town lattice covered bridge served the village of Brasher Falls. Elevated causeways led up to where it perched above the St. Regis River, high on stone abutments over a rocky ledge. Erected in 1863, it bore much trunk-line traffic across northern New York and a covered walkway was added on the downstream side for pedestrians. A modern span on U.S. Rt. 11 replaced it in 1933.
ST. LAWRENCE COUNTY　　　　　　　　　　　　　　　　　Cr. John L. Warner

At the village of Helena was a single-span arch and kingpost bridge over the Deer River. Typical of village bridges, it had an attached outside sidewalk. The Helena Bridge gave service for over three-quarters of a century; from 1855 to 1931. Destruction was by a dynamite blast.
ST. LAWRENCE COUNTY   Cr. Basil Kievit

The covered bridge over the log-filled Oswegatchie River on William Street in Gouverneur stood until 1892. It must have been a traumatic experience for horses to emerge from its south portal at the moment a train rumbled onto the trestle overhead.
ST. LAWRENCE COUNTY   Cr. Allen Collection

A long, two-span wooden arch bridge with "storm door" portals once spanned the Sacandaga River, connecting the villages of Edinburg and Batchellerville. Built by James Partridge in 1844, it stood until the creation of the Sacandaga Reservoir. On March 29, 1930, the old bridge was purposely burned.
SARATOGA COUNTY   Cr. Basil Kievit Collection

Just south of Hadley Village was a double-barrel arch bridge over the mouth of the Sacandaga River. Built in 1813 under the direction of Obadiah Wilcox, it was sheathed in wood in the form of an arch clear down to the base of the abutments. It was replaced in 1885 by an elliptical iron arch bridge which is itself an old landmark today.
SARATOGA COUNTY   Cr. Seneca Ray Stoddard

A view of the Sacandaga River railroad bridge at Hadley made in 1866. This shows the as-yet-unsheathed high bridge of the newly-build Adirondack Railway. It was a 518-foot wood-and-iron Howe Truss structure of four spans. Locomotive is the company's first, the "Maj. Gen Hancock."
SARATOGA COUNTY   Cr. Seneca Ray Stoddard

In 1885 the covered bridge over the Sacandaga River at Hadley was replaced by a unique "lenticular" truss of iron. It was fabricated by the Berlin Iron Bridge Company of Connecticut, and has its roadway suspended at the center of the elliptical truss. Locally known as "the bow bridge," it is approaching the century mark still carrying restricted loads.
SARATOGA COUNTY   Cr. Basil Kievit

Over a century ago, Arad Copeland had farm land on both sides of Beecher's Creek in Edinburg, just below Beecher's Hollow. In 1879 Copeland built this little covered bridge just for his cows to reach their upland pasture. It is a simple kingpost truss, twenty-nine feet long, and the sole survivor of the old important covered bridges which once dotted the Sacandaga Valley.
SARATOGA COUNTY   Cr. R. S. Allen Collection

An early covered wooden railroad bridge of the Rensselaer & Saratoga Railroad (D&H) spanned the Kayaderosseras Creek near the "Blue Mill" at Ballston Spa.
SARATOGA COUNTY   Cr. Allen Collection

Devised by the inventive genius Squire Whipple of Albany, this vertical lift bridge spanned the Champlain Canal on Broad Street in the village of Waterford. Canal boats had priority and when the bridge was open vehicular traffic came to a halt, while pedestrians used the wooden stairways. In the distance is the double passageway of the Waterford-Lansingburgh Bridge.
SARATOGA COUNTY   Cr. Frances D. Broderick Collection.

High water tore out the wooden center pier of the Hudson River Bridge at Glens Falls, but failed to dislodge the lattice structure. Erected in 1842, it withstood log jams and heavy traffic until replaced in 1890.
SARATOGA-WARREN COUNTIESCr. Seneca Ray Stoddard

Schenectady, from the West.

Schenectady's covered bridge across the Mohawk River was unique in the annals of bridge building. Here, in 1808–09 Theodore Burr devised and erected an unprecedented, un-covered wooden suspension bridge; its cables composed of huge laminated tiimbers. In use, the experimental structure sagged and additional piers had to be added. In order to protect the wooden suspension system, the bridge was covered in sections. Despite its weird, undulating appearance, it was used for seven years by cars of the pioneer Schenectady and Saratoga Railway.
SCHENECTADY COUNTY   Cr. Allen Collection

Cobblestoned Washington Avenue led to the old Schenectady-Scotia Toll Bridge over the Mohawk River. It was not replaced until 1874.
SCHENECTADY COUNTY
Cr. N. Berton Alter Collection

RATES OF TOLL.

Every Foot Passenger, — 3

Every head of live Sheep, Hogs or Calves, — 1½

Every head of Horned Cattle, — 9

Every Horse, Jack, Mule or Ox, whether led or drove, — 9

Every Horse or Mule and rider, — 12½

Every two wheel Pleasure Carriage, drawn by one Horse, 18¾
Jack or Mule,
and SIX CENTS for every additional Horse, Jack or Mule.

Every four wheel Pleasure Carriage, the body whereof is sup- 25
ported by springs or thorough-braces, drawn by one Horse, Jack or Mule,
and TWELVE AND A HALF CENTS for every additional Horse, Jack or Mule.

Every Pleasure Wagon, drawn by one Horse, Jack or Mule, 25
and TWELVE AND A HALF CENTS for every additional Horse, Jack or Mule.

Every Stage Wagon, drawn by one Horse, Jack or Mule, 18¾
and SIX AND A QUARTER CENTS for every additional 3d or 4th Horse, Jack or Mule.

Every Stage Wagon, drawn by five Horses, Jacks or Mules, 37
and TWENTY-FIVE CENTS for every further additional Horse, Jack or Mule.

Every Freight or Burthen Wagon, drawn by one Horse, 12½
Jack, Mule or Ox,
and SIX CENTS for every additional 3d, 4th or 5th Horse, Jack, Mule or Ox.
And for every further additional Horse, Jack, Mule or Ox, TWENTY-FIVE CENTS.

Every Cart or other two wheel Carriage of burthen, drawn 12½
by one Horse, Jack, Mule or Ox,
and SIX AND A QUARTER CENTS for every additional Horse, Jack, Mule or Ox.

Every Sleigh or Sled, of any description, drawn by one 12½
Horse, Jack, Mule or Ox,
and SIX AND A QUARTER CENTS for every additional Horse, Jack, Mule or Ox.

Fine of One Dollar,

For any person or persons crossing the Mohawk Bridge on Horse Back or in a Carriage or Sleigh of any description, to travel faster than on a walk, or

For any person to cross said Bridge with Horses, Jacks, Mules or Oxen, consisting of more than Ten in one Drove, or to cross with Loaded Carriages or Sleighs drawn by more than two beasts, at a less distance than 30 feet, each from the other, or

For any person or persons with Carriage or Carriages, Sleigh or Sleighs of any description, or with any kind of Beasts to take the left hand passage.

5000 Dollars Fine for attempting to injure or destroy said Bridge.

Rates of Toll on Schenectady's Mohawk Bridge were detailed and precise. It was up to the toll-taker to collect—or drop his gate.
SCHENECTADY COUNTY   Cr. Allen Collection

Early on, the railroads endeavored to put reliance on iron rather than wood for their bridges. At Schenectady was an early experimental bridge truss of the 1850's, an iron lattice first developed in the British Isles. This unique double-track, triple-truss bridge, built on a decided skew, carried the rails of the New York Central over the Erie Canal, on what is now Erie Boulevard.
SCHENECTADY COUNTY   Cr. Allen Collection

This 56-foot iron arch truss bears the nameplate: "S. WHIPPLE'S PATENT, SHIPMAN & SON, BUILDERS, SPRINGFIELD CENTRE, N.Y." It formerly spanned Cayadutta Creek in Johnstown, Fulton County. In 1979 three engineering students at Union College conceived the project of dismantling the bridge and re-erecting it for pedestrian usage on the Union College campus in Schenectady. Accomplished with the help of a small financial grant the following year, the bridge is a memorial to its inventor, Squire Whipple, a member of Union's Class of 1830.
SCHENECTADY COUNTY   Cr. R. S. Allen

Barely discernible in this old Stoddard view of the upper Hudson River is the covered bridge which spanned it at the way station called "The Glen," above Warrensburg.
WARREN COUNTY   Cr. Seneca Ray Stoddard

As the Adirondack Mountains began to be exploited for their lumber and tan bark, it was felt that a bridge was necessary to span the upper Hudson River west of Chestertown. Accordingly, in 1870 the "Folsom Landing Central Bridge Company" was formed as a private enterprise; a further reason for being was to reach the new Adirondack Railway on the west bank. The site is today known as Riverside, or Riparius. In quest of lucrative tolls, the company proceeded to erect a 308-foot wood-and-wire cable suspension bridge across the Hudson, at a cost of some $15,000.
WARREN COUNTY   Cr. Seneca Ray Stoddard

Fulson Landing Bridge, Riparius, Adirondacks, N.Y.:
Only Suspension Bridge on Hudson River

At Riverside, the long wire cables hung from the massive wooden towers for forty-five years. Long before the building of the Bear Mountain and George Washington bridges over the lower river, this span was noted as "the only suspension bridge on the Hudson." Toll collecting finally came to an end, and a new, free steel arch bridge was erected in 1919–20.
WARREN COUNTY   Cr. Allen Collection

Skeleton of newly-built wooden Howe Truss bridge of the Adirondack Railway spans Stony Creek just above its junction with the Hudson River. Later protected from the weather, this sturdy span served from 1865 to 1891.
WARREN COUNTY   Cr. Seneca Ray Stoddard

On the main road between Cambridge, N.Y. and Arlington, Vt. was Gainer's Bridge over the Batten Kill. Built by Caleb Orcutt in 1840, the Town lattice span served New Yorkers and Vermonters until 1934.
WASHINGTON COUNTY

Cr. Allen Collection

Eagleville (or "East Salem") still has a covered bridge across the Batten Kill, built in 1858 by Ephraim W. Clapp. A long Town lattice single span, it is situated to the west of Rt. 313, the New York State highway between Cambridge and Arlington, Vt.
WASHINGTON COUNTY

Cr. Lee Wolff

Shushan Bridge as it appeared when carrying traffic. Built over the Batten Kill in 1858 by Milton and James C. Stevens, this bridge served Shushan village for over a century. With the erection of a new high level crossing, the old lattice span was moved slightly, placed on a new concrete foundation, and is today preserved and locally-maintained as a museum.
WASHINGTON COUNTY Cr. Allen Collection

Three miles out of Salem is the former village of Rexleigh, marked today only by a broken dam, a crumbled mill and a covered bridge. At one time the site of flourishing marble quarries and an edged tool-making establishment, the Batten Kill was spanned here in 1874 by a 100-foot Howe Truss bridge, probably erected by builder/inventor Reuben Comins of Troy. Comins used his patented cast iron "shoes" to make seats for the butt ends of the bridge timbers, and this rare wrinkle in covered bridge building can still be seen at Rexleigh. Now painted red and white, the bridge has been closed for some time, a bone of contention between modernists and exponents of historic preservation. This photo dates from the 1930's prior to full housing and re-painting.
WASHINGTON COUNTY Cr. Allen Collection

South of Salem, present-day N.Y. Rt. 22 crosses the Batten Kill on the site of "Red Bridge," a horizontally-boarded lattice span. Built by Washington County's covered bridge builder Caleb Orcutt in 1858, it was washed out in the Great Flood of 1927, and dismantled in a field downstream.
WASHINGTON COUNTY   Cr. Allen Collection

At Union Village (now Greenwich) an early lattice bridge crossed the Batten Kill. It is depicted to the left in this old woodcut, made prior to 1842.
WASHINGTON COUNTY   Cr. Allen Collection

The small mill town of Battenville had its own covered bridge over the Batten Kill. It followed the lattice truss pattern so widely used in the area, with the addition of strengthening auxiliary arches.
WASHINGTON COUNTY   Cr. Allen Collection

Today's Middle Falls on the Batten Kill was formerly the mill village of Galesville. Its single-span Howe truss covered bridge was succeeded by a concrete arch in 1915.
WASHINGTON COUNTY Cr. Allen Collection

Over the Owl Kill, east of N.Y. Rt. 22 and the village of Center White Creek was "Sheehy's" or "Red Bridge," with a 45-foot Town lattice truss. Taken over by Washington County in 1938, the little span was renovated and given a new red and white paint job. Unhappily, this new lease on life was punctuated when overloading and broken lower chords brought replacement in 1953.
WASHINGTON COUNTY   Photo by R. S. Allen

Called "Carpenter's Bridge," this little 46-foot Town lattice span once carried traffic on a short cut across the Owl Kill east of Eagle Bridge. When a viaduct to carry N.Y. Rt. 67 was erected in 1932, the bridge and a dangerous railroad grade crossing beyond were abandoned. Grown up with vines, the old span endured another 15 years, and was demolished for its lumber in October, 1947.
WASHINGTON COUNTY   Photo by R. S. Allen

Sluggish Wood Creek is part of the ancient water level route between the Champlain and Hudson Valleys. Just south of Whitehall the stream was spanned by Howe Truss covered bridges. That on the Rutland & Washington Railroad dated from 1850, and the highway bridge on Poultney Street was built in 1877. This last, a single span of 150 feet, is shown here with covering removed, prior to canalization of Wood Creek in 1915.
WASHINGTON COUNTY   Cr. Allen Collection

Shared with the Green Mountain State was the Carver's Falls bridge between Hampton and Fair Haven, Vt. In March, 1940, an ice jam in the Poultney River lifted it off its abutments, and it was purposely burned on the ice to protect a power plant below.
WASHINGTON CO., N.Y.-RUTLAND COUNTY, VT.   Cr. Allen Collection

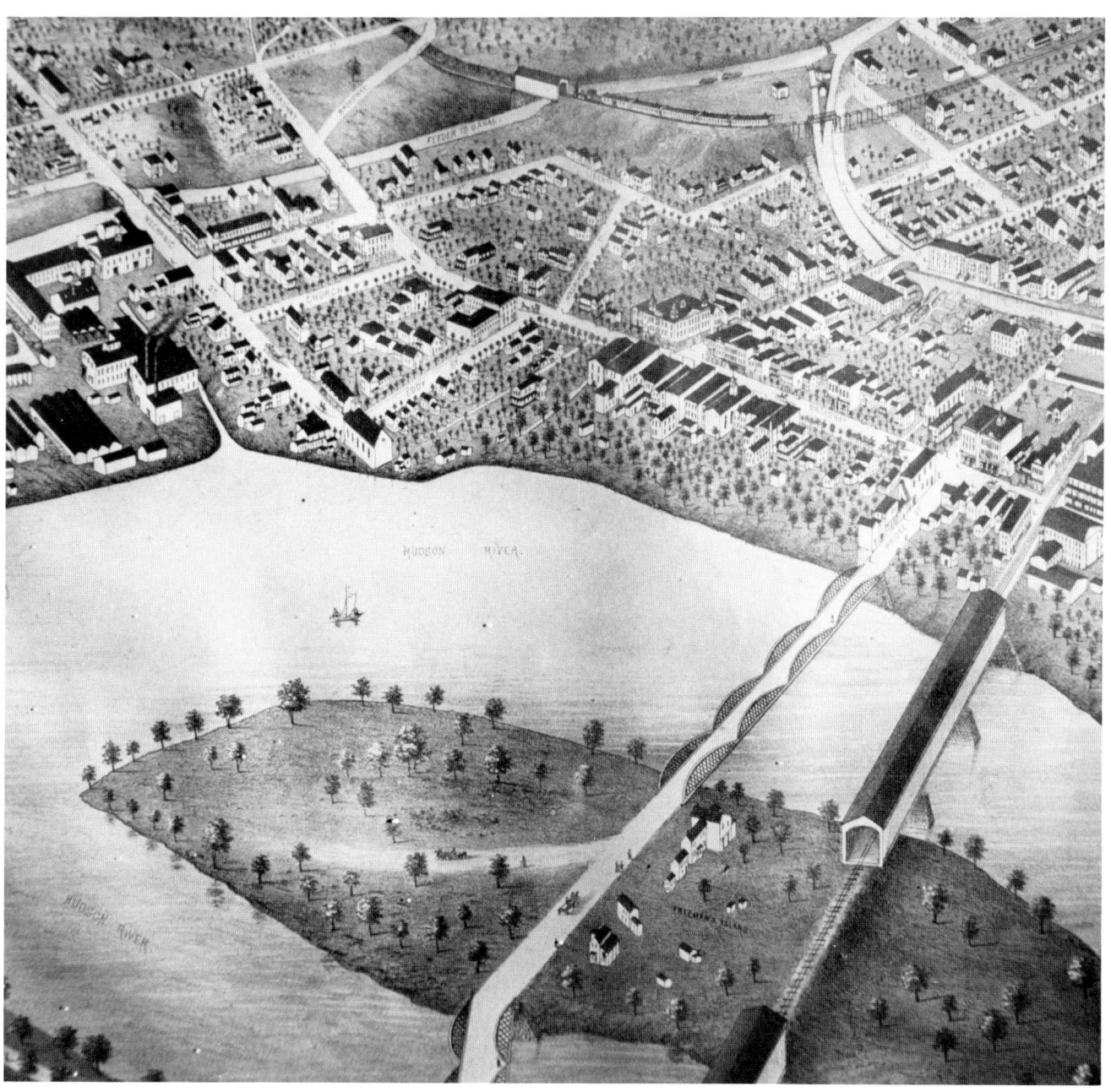

After numerous financial troubles, the Saratoga & Washington Rail Road (D&H) was extended to Whitehall in 1848. Two covered bridges, divided by an island in the Hudson River, brought the tracks into Fort Edward. This bird's eye view of the 1870's shows the Fort Edward Blast Furnace (left) and (top) another covered railroad bridge for the Glens Falls Branch line, over the Feeder Canal. The twins over the Hudson were replaced in 1876.
SARATOGA-WASHINGTON COUNTIES   Cr. Sally Brillon, Washington County Historian

The KINGPOST truss for SHORT SPANS

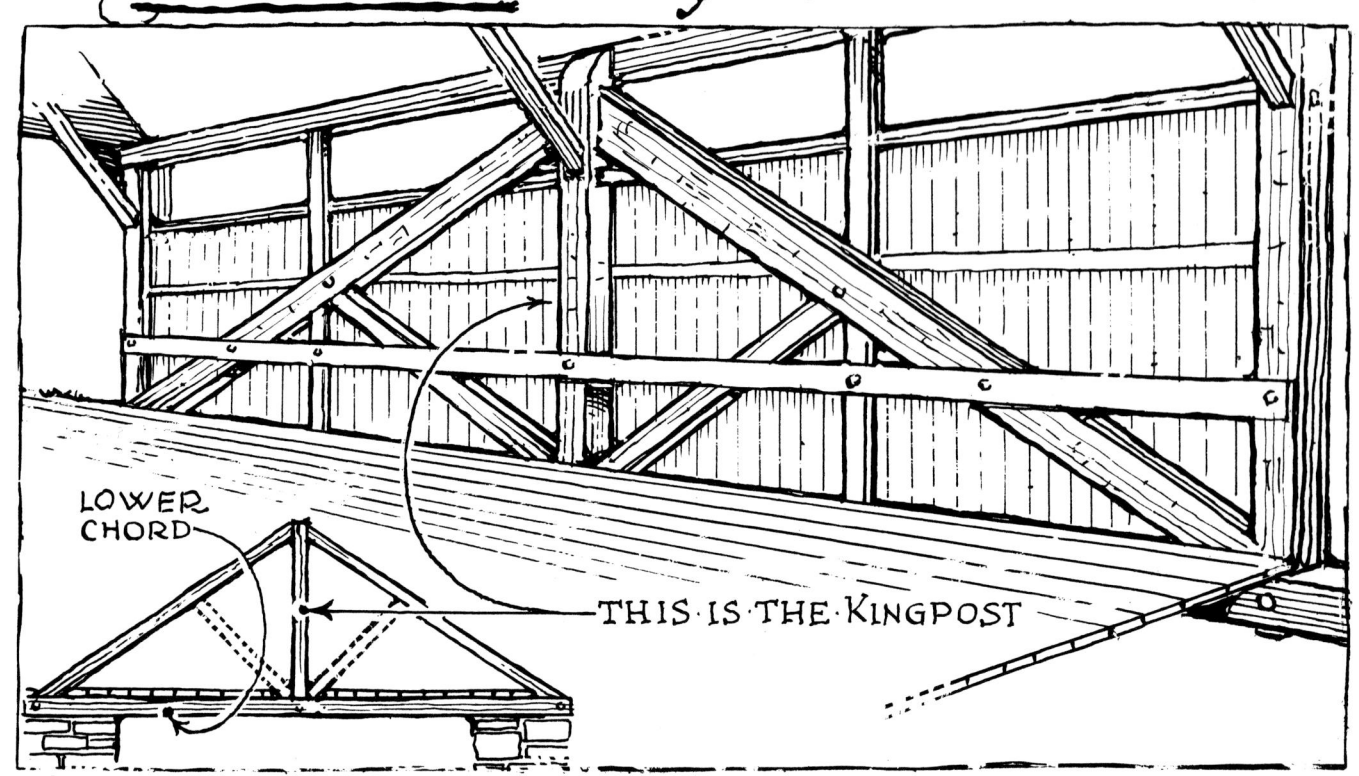

LOWER CHORD

THIS IS THE KINGPOST

and by adding another upright, you have a QUEENPOST Truss for Longer Spans

UPPER CHORD
LOWER CHORD
Queenposts

These following four drawings illustrate wooden bridge trusses typical of those built for the major covered bridges of northern New York State.

Courtesy of Eric Sloane

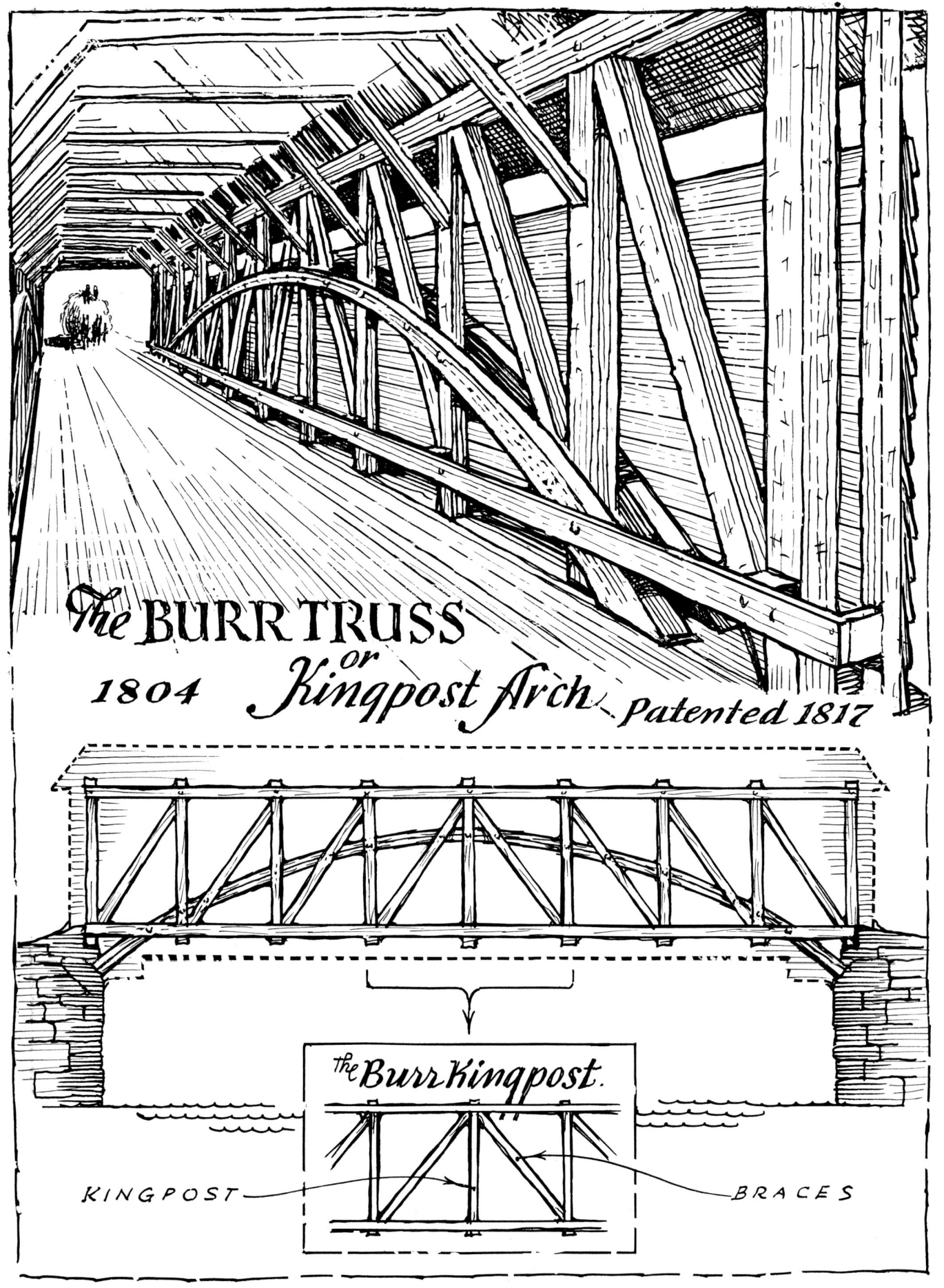

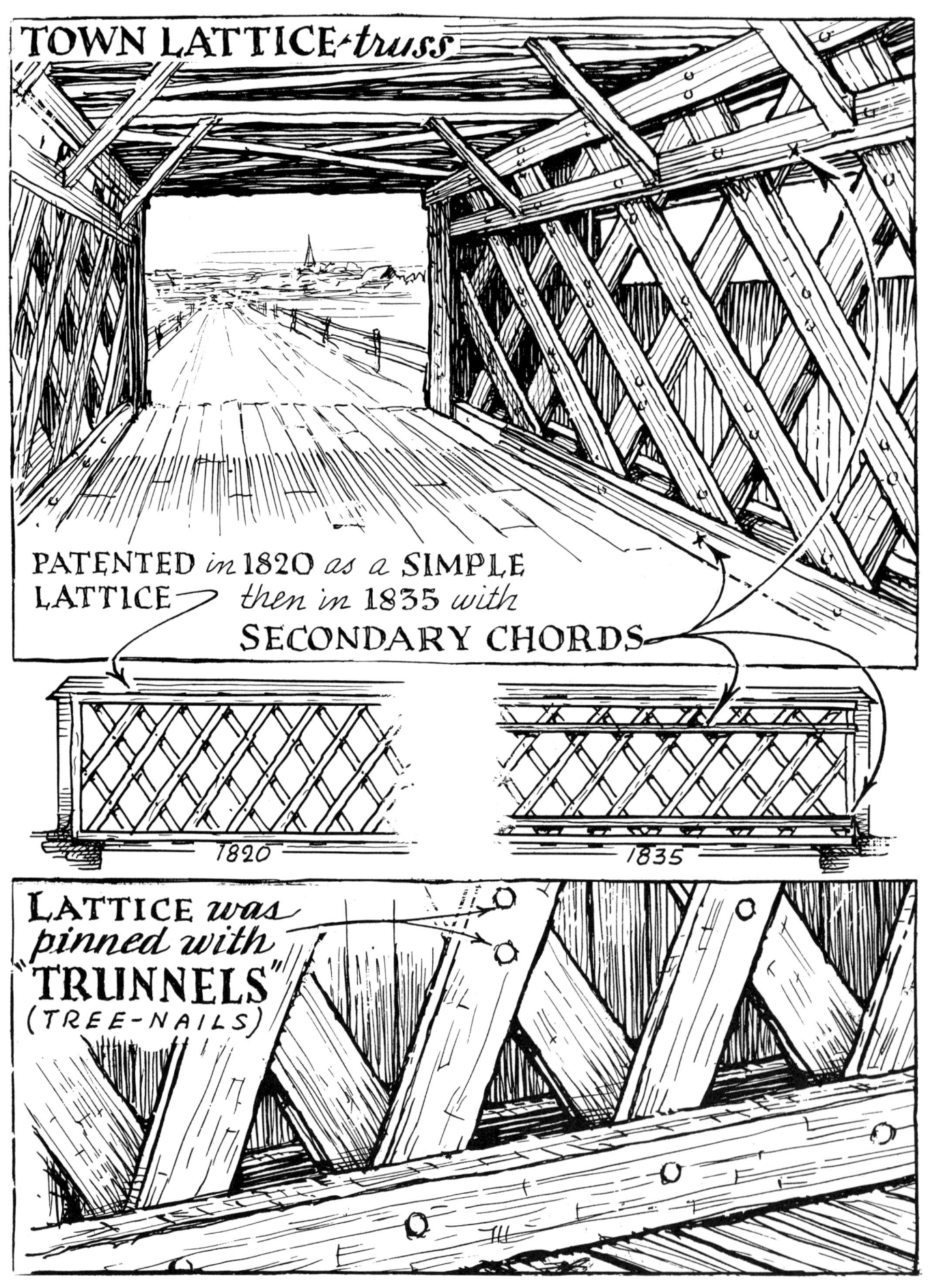

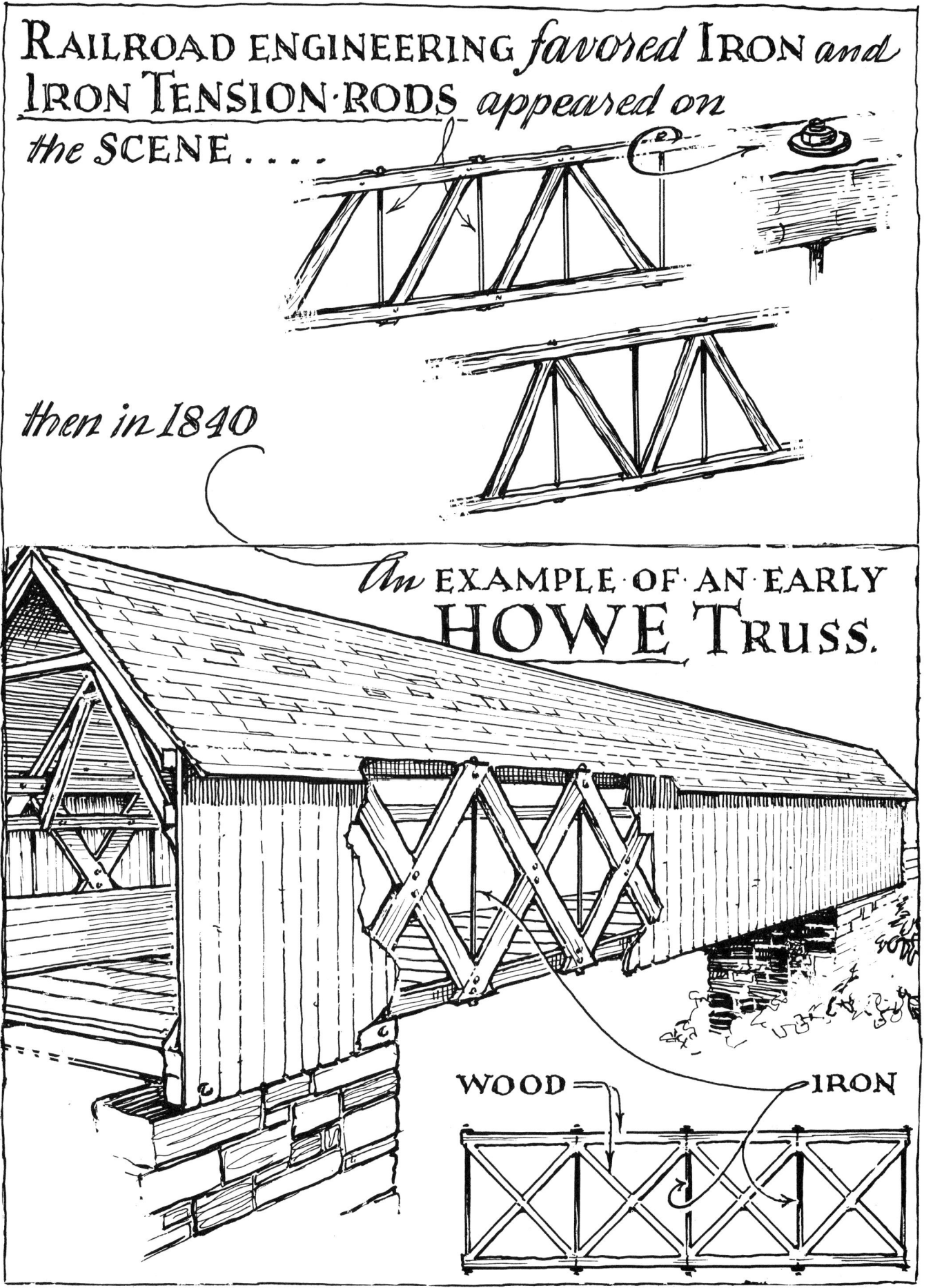

Existing Covered Wooden Bridges

Jay	Essex County	East Branch, Ausable River	Howe Truss	4–150″ 1857
Salisbury Center	Herkimer Co.	Spruce Creek	Burr Truss	1–42′ 1875
Buskirk	Rensselaer-Washington Cos.	Hoosic River	Howe Truss	1–165′ c. 1880
Edinburg	Saratoga County (Private)	Beecher Creek	Queenpost	1–29′ 1879
Eagleville	Washington County	Batten Kill	Town Lattice	1–88′ 1858
Shushan	Washington County (Preserved)	Batten Kill	Town Lattice	2–160′ 1858
Rexleigh	Washington County (Closed)	Batten Kill	Howe Truss	1–100′ 1874

Some Existing Old Iron Bridges

Normans Kill Farm	Albany County	Trib. of Norman's Kill	Whipple Iron Arch	1–111′ 1867
Keeseville	Clinton-Essex Counties	Ausable River	Wire Cable Suspension	1–240′ 1888
North of Fonda	Montgomery County	Cayadutta Creek	Whipple Iron Arch	1–72′ 1869
Hadley	Saratoga County	Sacandaga River	Berlin Lenticular	1–135′ 1885
Union College	Schenectady Co.	Hans Groot's Kill	Whipple Iron Arch	1–56′ c. 1860

An Index for "Old North Country Bridges"

Adirondack Railway, 85, 93, 94
Albany, 10
Albany & Vermont Railroad, 14, 72
Albany Northern Railroad, 18
Albany, Vermont & Canada Railroad, 72
Allendale, 45
Amsterdam, 52, 53
Arlington, Vt., 95, 96
Ausable River, 19, 20, 22–23, 24, 25

Ballston Spa, 87
Batchellerville, 83
Batten Kill, 95, 96, 97, 98, 99, 100
Battenville, 99
Beecher's Creek, 86
Belden & Gale, 18
Bennington Battlefield (N.Y.), 69
Berlin Bridge Company, 22, 24, 86
Black River, 44, 46
Boston & Maine Railroad, 70, 71
Bradford, Gilbert, 46
Bradford Suspension Bridge, 46
Brasher Falls, 80
Brockett's Bridge, 34
Burr, Theodore, 41, 50, 73, 90
Buskirk's Bridge, 77

Cambridge, 95, 96
Cameron Bridge, 43
Campbell, Henry R., 29
Canajoharie, 50, 57
Canton, 79
Caroga Creek, 55
Carpenter's Bridge 101
Carver's Falls, 102
Caughnawaga Bridge, 51
Cayadutta Creek, 56, 57
Center White Creek, 101
Champlain Canal, 15, 88
Chateaugay, 27

Chateaugay River, 27
Chestertown, 93
Cincinnatus Creek, 60
Clapp, Ephraim W., 96
Cohoes, 15, 16–17, 18
Comins, Reuben, 97
Congdon, John, 28
Copeland, Arad, 86
Countryman's (Dempster's) Bridge, 36
Court Street Bridge (Watertown), 44
Crooks, Harry F., 30

Damon, Isaac, 12–13, 15
Deer River, 81
De Graff, Simon, 10
Dolgeville, 34

Eagle Bridge, 76, 101
Eagle Mills, 68
Eagleville (East Salem), 96
East Canada Creek, 33, 34, 41
Edinburg, 83, 86
Ellisburg, 45
Elwell's Falls Bridge, 38
Emmonsburg, 33
Ephratah, 55
Erie Canal, 8, 54, 57, 92

Fair Haven (Vt.), 102
Fink's Bridge, 40
Fish House, 33
Fish House Bridge, 31, 32
Folsom Landing Central Bridge Company, 93
Fonda, 51, 56
Fort Edward, 103
Fort Hunter, 52
Fort Plain, 47, 48–49
Fox Creek, 11
French's Hollow Bridge, 5, 6
Fultonville, 51, 54

Gainer's Bridge, 95
Galesville (Middle Falls), 100
Gang Mills Bridge, 41
Gardner, Robert, 61
German Church Road Bridge, 36
Glen, 54
Glens Falls, 89
Glens Falls Branch Railroad, 103
Glens Falls Feeder Canal, 103
Gouverneur, 82
Grasse River, 79
Gravesville, 43
Green Island, 12–13
Green Island Bridge, 12–13, 14
Greenwich, 98
Guilderland, 4
Guilderland Center, 5

Hadley, 84, 85, 86
Hampton, 102
Haupt, Herman, 46
Hayward, Joseph, 12–13, 15, 22
Helena, 81
Herkimer, 36
Hinckley, 41
Hogansburg, 26
Hoosic River, 61, 62, 76, 77
Hoosick, 62
Hoosick & White Creek Bridge Company, 76
Hoosick Bridge, 61
Hoosick Falls, 62
Hopson, Alvah, 36, 37, 38, 39
Howe, William, 77
Hudson River, 12–13, 72, 73, 89, 93, 94, 102, 103

Jay Bridge, 25

Kayaderosseras Creek, 87
Kinney's Creek, 78

109

Keeseville, 19, 20, 21, 22, 24
Lansingburgh, 74–75, 88
Little Falls, 40
Little Hoosic River, 63, 64–65, 66
Little Salmon River, 28
Log London Bridge, 45
Lorraine, 45
Lyonsdale, 46

Malone, 29
Massena Center, 78
Middle Falls, 100
Mohawk River, 15, 16–17, 18, 40, 41, 47, 48–49, 50, 51, 52, 53, 90, 91
Moore's Mill Bridge, 37
Moose River, 46
Murphy, John W., 52
Murray, Dougal & Co., 20

Nelliston, 47
New Scotland, 7, 9
New York Central Railroad, 58–59, 92
Norman's Kill, 5, 7
Norman's Kill Farm Bridge, 10
Northampton, 31, 33
Northern Railroad, 29
North Hoosick, 69
North Petersburg, 66, 76
North Pownal (Vt.), 76

Oakwood Cemetery Bridge, 70, 71
Orcutt, Caleb, 95, 98
Osborn's Bridge, 30
Oswegatchie River, 82
Otsquago Creek, 47
Owl Kill, 101

Palatine Bridge, 50, 57
Partridge, James, 83
Petersburg, 63, 64–65

Poesten Kill, 68
Poland, 44
Port Jackson, 52
Post, Simeon S., 18
Poultney River, 102
Prospect, 42

Red Bridge (Salem), 98
Red (Sheehy's) Bridge, 101
Rensselaer & Saratoga Railroad, 12–13, 87
Remsen, 60
Rexleigh, 97
Riparius (Riverside), 93, 94
Roebling, John A., 52
Rome, 58–59
Rutland & Washington Railroad, 102

Sacandaga River, 30, 31, 35, 83, 84, 85, 86
Saint Johnsville, 41, 47
Saint Regis River, 26, 80
Salem, 97, 98
Salisbury, 36, 37
Salisbury Center, 38, 39
Salmon River, 29
Sandy Creek, (S. Branch), 45
Saratoga & Washington Railroad, 72, 103
Schaghticoke Hill, 67
Schlatter, Col. Charles L., 29
Schenectady, 90, 91, 92
Schenectady & Utica Railway, 50
Scotia Toll Bridge, 90
Sharp's Corners, 4
Shedd's Bridge, 69
Shipman & Son, 92
Shushan, 97
Slimser, Henry, Farm Bridge, 54

South Bombay, 28
Spruce Creek, 36, 37, 38, 39
State Line Bridge, 76
Stevens, Milton & James C., 97
Stewart, Daniel, 31
Stillwater, 72
Stony Creek, 94

The Glen, 93
Tomhannock Creek, 67
Townsend, Soloman, 22
Trenton Falls Bridge, 42
Troy, 12–13, 70, 71
Troy & Boston Railroad, 62

Union Bridge, 74–75
Union Village (Greenwich), 98

Van Auken, J. P. S., 4
Vlaie Creek, 33
Vly Creek, 9

Wagner's Hollow Bridge, 55
Waldbillig Bridge, 9
Waldbillig, Gerald, 9
Walden, Gen. Hiram, 11
Waldenville, 11
Walloomsac River, 69
Warrensburg, 93
Waterford, 72, 73, 74–75, 88
Watertown, 44, 46
Watervliet, 8
Wells, 35
Wells' Bridge (Petersburg), 64–65
West Canada Creek, 36, 41, 42, 43, 44
Whipple, Squire, 43, 56, 57, 88, 92
Whitehall, 102
Wilcox, Obadiah, 84
Witherwax, Henry, 5
Wood Creek, 102